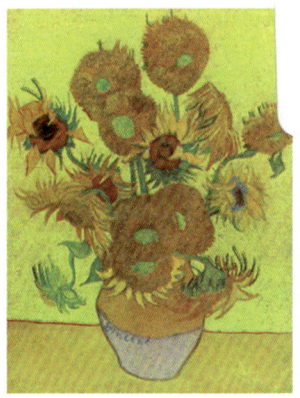

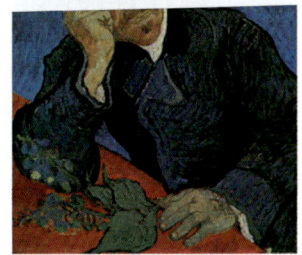

VAN GOGH
Sunflowers

VAN GOGH
Portrait of Dr. Gachet

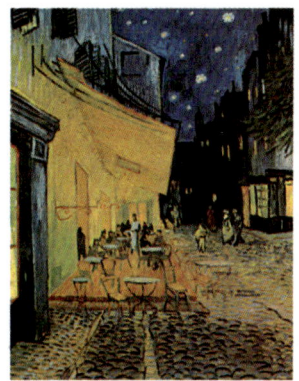

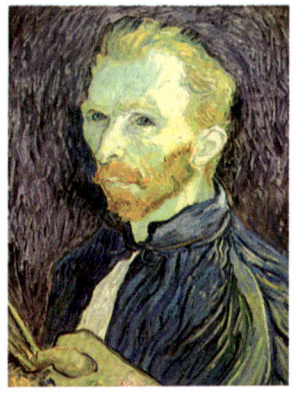

VAN GOGH
Café Terrace by Night

VAN GOGH
Self-Portrait

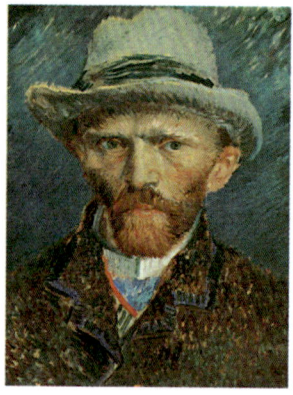

V A N   G O G H
Self-Portrait with Gray Hat

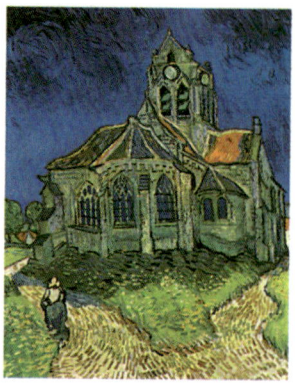

V A N   G O G H
The Church at Auvers

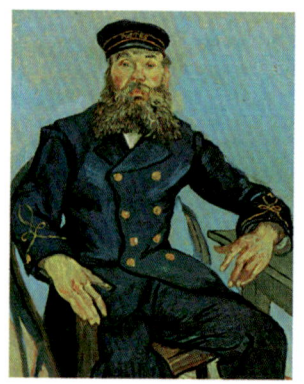

V A N   G O G H
The Postman Roulin

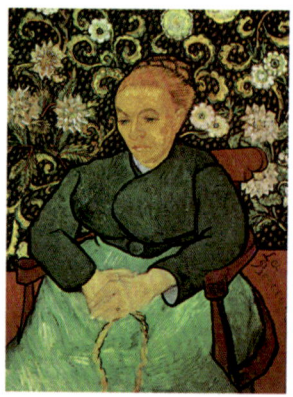

V A N   G O G H
La Berceuse (Augustine Roulin)

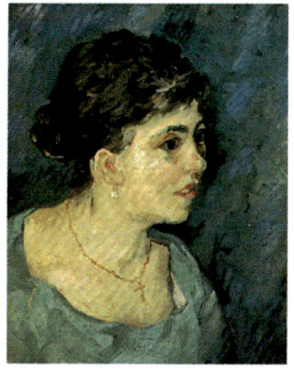

VAN GOGH
Portrait of a Woman in Blue

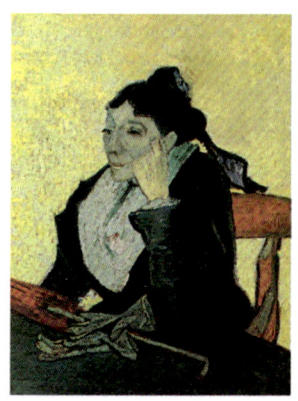

VAN GOGH
L'Arlésienne, Mme. Ginoux

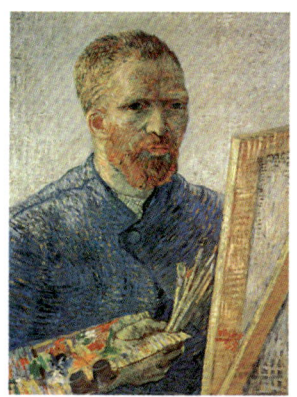

VAN GOGH
Self-Portrait of the Artist at Work

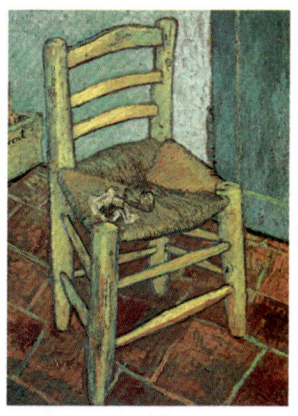

VAN GOGH
Vincent's Chair

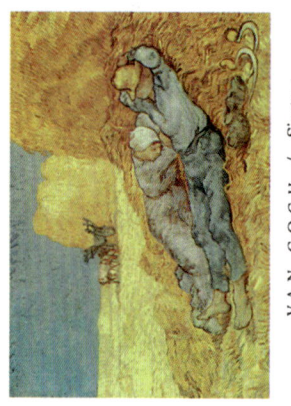

VAN GOGH / Siesta

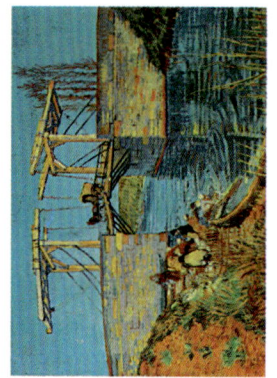

VAN GOGH / The Bridge at Langlois

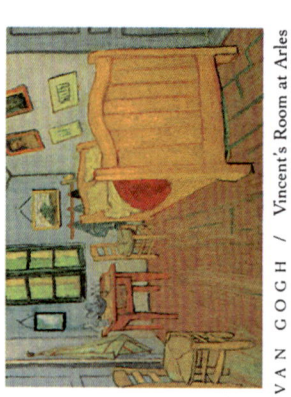

VAN GOGH / Vincent's Room at Arles

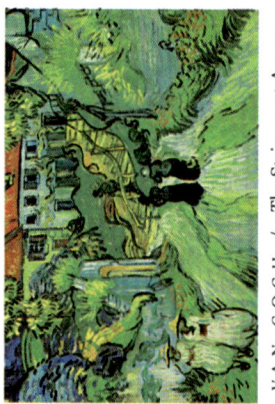

VAN GOGH / The Staircase at Auvers

40395-5